THE SANDWICH ISLANDS

AS THEY ARE,

NOT AS THEY SHOULD BE.

BY MRS. E. M. WILLS PARKER.

SAN FRANCISCO:

BURGESS, GILBERT & STILL,
PORTSMOUTH SQUARE.

PRINTED AT THE DISPATCH JOB OFFICE, COMMERCIAL STREET, COR. LEIDESDORFF.

PREFACE.

My only excuse for giving these hasty sketches to the public must be, the thousand questions I am daily asked regarding the Sandwich Islands, since my return from them, and the general desire manifested by the community, just at this time, to know something definite of their past and present history. I have been stimulated also by a sense of duty to society, to expose the monstrous deception which has so long imposed upon the world, and especially upon those whose truthfulness and purity would prevent a suspicion of duplicity in others. At least, I trust an investigation may be the result of these developments, which ought long since to have been made by a bolder and more skilful hand than my own.

E. M. W. PARKER.

SAN FRANCISCO, *February*, 1852.

THE

SANDWICH ISLANDS AS THEY ARE,

NOT AS THEY SHOULD BE.

We left San Francisco on the 12th of November, 1851, to visit the Sandwich Islands, and perhaps spend the anticipated "rainy season" in the fair city of Honolulu. The smart little craft in which we were embarked made good the quiet boast of her captain, who "Guessed she was as fast as any of 'em," and on the morning of the 26th, landed us safe at the little town of Lahaina, on the island of Mauie. No terrible hurricane converted the smooth surface of the lazy deep into mountains and valleys, or rural scenery of any kind; no hidden rocks threatened us, that we know of, and if the mighty monsters of the deep *did* "wag their tails about," they were so far under water that they never raised a ripple on the surface. Fair skies and fair winds favored us, and when, one evening, the helmsman went to sleep, and the mast and the monotony were nearly broken together, we felt it rather an agreeable episode. The evening of the 25th found us running along the island of Owyhee, which lay like an immense shadow on our left, draped in clouds, the mighty volcano of Kirauea rearing its head far above into the pale moonlight; but Pele, the native goddess of the volcano, must have put out her fires for the night, for not a spark, or even a puff of smoke issued from any one of her fifty craters. All night, on the smoothest of seas, and under the loveliest skies, we floated, and just when dawn blushes into day, entered the port of Lahaina. Rosy clouds rested on the mountain-tops, and a gauzy mist filled the valley, through which, dimly seen, arose a solitary spire, a few masts, and the plumed heads of cocoanut trees, standing like a guard of Maltese knights, over some conquered hamlet. But when the sun rose, and dissolved the illusion, we saw before us a lovely bay of sparkling water, upon the shores of which a village nestled beneath the shade of the palm, bread-fruit, and orange trees, now in their rich winter foliage. In the background, apparently forming an impenetrable barrier to the interior, rose precipitously a chain of high, sharp-pointed hills, seamed and torn by the waterfalls which plunge down their sides at some seasons of the year, carrying wonderful fertilization into the vale below. Here coffee grows wild in abundance, and we plucked a pod of silky cotton from an indigénous plant *twelve feet* high! The interior of the island contains plantations rich with all the products of the torrid zone, but the land near the town lies quite uncultivated, the natives living on raw fish and poe, and the fruits which are indigenous to the soil, and the foreigners being supplied with vegetables and meats from the plantations on the other side of the island. The town consists of a few good wooden houses, and a great many tumble-down turf and grass hovels, filled with naked and half covered natives, who seem to divide their time equally between squatting on their heels, and playing in the sea. Men, women, children, and infants, tumbling, rolling, screaming, and laughing in the water, formed the only animated scene we witnessed; for all the whale-ships had departed, which visit Lahaina in the spring and fall, and the sultry silence of a tropical mid-day seemed to have settled upon the place. Hot, hot upon our devoted heads shone the sun, as we took our seats in a boat sheltered by a cotton awning, to go to the very comfortable hotel of the place; the sea was one glare of light, and the rays, reflected from the sparkling sand and shells of the beach, were almost intolerable.

We were surrounded in our progress by a whole fleet of native canoes, all soliciting passengers; but no one felt disposed to risk himself in a boat like the half of a sharp-pointed cucumber, in which the owners themselves sat like so many bronze statues, the movement of paddling coming from their arms only, and not at all affecting their bodies. Landed, we hastened to pay our respects to the American consul, Mr. Bunker, who fully maintains his character for kindness and urbanity. He and his daughter occupy a charming residence, but find the place extremely dull for persons of their literary tastes and attainments. After an excellent dinner at the hotel, of beef, fowls in variety, vegetables, fruits, custards, &c., we sallied out to explore the town, which lies in a narrow strip, for a quarter of a mile along the bay. What would be thought squalid poverty anywhere else, seems to bring the fullness of content to the simple natives. A hut built of turf or matting, two calabashes, and a plate of wood for poe, with a few mats to sleep and lounge on, form the whole furniture of residences, where pigs, children, goats, and fowls live in perfect and most filthy harmony.

As we sauntered along, we came upon a group taking their evening meal, and stopped to observe them. A half dozen, of different ages and sexes, were seated flat on the ground, in a circle around two calabashes, one containing poe, and the other fish, just captured, for supper, and still convulsively leaping and writhing about, unconscious of what was to come. We looked in vain for any fire to cook them, when, to our horror, a flat-nosed young beauty of sixteen seized a horrible cuttle-fish, and, striking her white, sharp teeth into it, was in an instant deluged in the blood and black juice of the creature, which wreathed its long tentaculæ about her head and face, till she almost petrified us into stone, as did her prototype, the Gorgon of old.

Poe is a thick paste made from the taro, a plant somewhat resembling the yam, and quite palatable when fried. The natives are exceedingly fond of it, and prefer it to all foreign delicacies. Their mode of eating it is peculiar, and not at all tempting. A large calabash of the paste is made, and allowed to ferment slightly; around this, any number less than twenty squat upon their feet, and in turn dip one or two fingers of the right hand, according to the consistence of the dish; one-fingered poe being much thicker than two-fingered poe. With a sudden twirl, it is wound around the fingers, the head is thrown back, when, plop! it goes into the immense aperture gaping to receive it, and in an instant disappears forever. It is a very nourishing diet, as the broad, shining faces of the natives testify, and while fatness continues among these people, as well as among the Mahometans, to be the criterion of beauty, it must continue to be held in high esteem.

We sauntered back to our hotel under the shade of the trees bordering the street, and saw hundreds of natives in every variety of indolence, but not one occupied, except it might be a mother, lazily searching the head of her shaggy offspring. We are apt to associate something of romance with the inhabitants of the Pacific isles, especially after reading Melville's happy delineations; but I have looked in vain for his noble warriors, or graceful Fayaway, in the wide-mouthed, flat-nosed creatures around me, whose only beauty is grossness, and only expression, sensuality. We left Lahaina the same evening, in the midst of a gorgeous sunset, and gliding on through the entire night before the coquettish winds of the Islands, only came in sight of Honolulu at daylight, though the distance is but sixty miles between the islands of Mauie and Oahu. Then a dead calm fell upon us, and we could not make the harbor until eleven o'clock, A. M., at which we were quite disappointed, as it was the day on which the people of the Sandwich Islands celebrate their independence, as guarantied by the English and French; but which guaranty, by the way, as is acknowledged now by all parties, was never made; each party only engaging not to interfere with the rights of the other. But it was otherwise understood, and it has now become a custom for the king to hold a levee upon that day, when all foreigners who wish can be presented at court, and polish their manners in an atmosphere of murky majesty they will not soon forget.

We could not get on shore in season to pay our respects to Kamehameha's queen, who held the levee in the place of His Majesty, then absent on a tour of his dominions; but from the account of a friend who was there, it has been admirably described by Lieutenant Price, in his "Los Gringos," except that he omitted to mention an *open secretary of old bonnets*, which forms one of the principal ornaments of the royal drawing-rooms. The harbor of Honolulu is pretty, though not large. It is defended from the sea by a coral reef, which encloses it, except one narrow channel, through which all vessels must enter and depart. The town presents a pleasing appearance as you approach. It consists of a goodly number of large airy houses, surrounded by deep verandahs, and embowered in shade trees of rich and profuse luxuriance. It had rained in the morning, and when we landed the air was perfumed with the geranium, jessamine, and other sweets, most grateful to our sea-nostrils. The wharf swarmed with natives, both male and female, in holiday attire; and here I noticed the difference between the provincials and the people of the metropolis. Whereas, at Lahaina, they were content with a single garment, and sometimes only half of one, and without ornament, here gaudy handkerchiefs were tied around the head, or suspended by the two opposite corners so as to fall in a square down the back; some wore gay wreaths around both head and neck, and some of the more extravagant wore shoes. They are very fond of sporting parasols, and you will often see a brawny fellow of six feet, with no garment but a shirt by no means too long, delicately defending his head with a sun-shade of half a yard in diameter.

The town is laid out in squares, and the streets are wide, and of fine, pleasant gravel, which is a mixture of coral and crushed lava. There are four churches, and plenty of stores and hotels; but the most agreeable residences are in the valleys in rear of the town, and the most luxurious of these belong to the missionaries. Would that some of the pious poor who, in a far-off land, have joyously contributed their hard-earned mite to the support of the "poor missionaries," could see their luxurious houses, filled with native slaves, for they are nothing more, and witness the idle luxury of their lives. My blood stirs with indignation as I contemplate the unblushing effrontery of these people, who send their whining beggars around the world, asking alms, in Christ's name, to contribute to the pleasures of their own useless existence! Let those who read their canting reports in the religious papers of the day, go to the Sandwich Islands, and see for themselves what has been done for the "barbarous natives." After the immense amount of money expended, and the wonderful accounts of revivals and reformations which have reached them, but which only exist in the brains of the inventors, they would have a right to expect, at least, an ordinary degree of morality and decorum; while, I will venture to say, that there is not another so corrupt and debased a people on the face of the earth, as the natives of the Sandwich Islands at this moment! Accomplished thieves and servile liars, from whom nothing but fear ever compels the truth, they have not the most distant idea of chastity, and I doubt if they have any word in their language to express it. Their licentiousness is incredible; and the child of eleven years is as deeply corrupted as the courtesan of twenty! I speak of no isolated cases, but of the whole Kanaka community; and they defend it by saying "It is no harm!" Poor wretches! their sin has overtaken them, for they are dying off at the rate of twenty per cent. annually. A few years, and the race will be extinct forever, and these lovely islands, — who but the missionaries will possess them? We shall see!

They have songs of so indecent a character, and dances, performed naked, so horrible, that they are not even named by foreign ladies; and no white mother will permit her child to learn the native tongue, lest it should become totally depraved by listening to their conversation. These facts, incredible as they seem, I have from foreign residents, and even the missionaries themselves. The most important changes which the missionaries have effected are, inducing the natives to go to church, and to wear bonnets; and even of the latter they made a good speculation, for they purchased them in Boston for a shilling apiece, and sold them to the natives for three and five dollars, imposing a fine on all females who did not wear a bonnet in church. All the finest property, and the best houses on the Islands are owned by missionaries and those banded with them. True, they deserve some compensation for their tremendous sacrifices! Have they not left poverty, an inhospitable climate, and an insignificant position, *to come away out here* to an earthly Paradise, where they roll in ease and luxury? In 1820, the first missionaries landed at Honolulu, and by their own account, published in the Missionary Herald, found a people ignorant, but innocent, brave and amiable. "They had already destroyed their idols, by the command of their king Rihoriho, son of the noble Kamehameha 1st, who was a man of ambitious spirit, and great powers, both of mind and body." They were a fine athletic race, their pleasures were innocent, they were contented with the position God had given them, and asked only to be left to the enjoyment of an unrivalled climate, and the spontaneous productions of Nature, their bounteous mother.

What is the result of thirty years of missionary labor? Diseased, powerless, degraded, the people have sunk into the position of slaves, nor dare they raise a hand in opposition, so complete is the bondage in which they are held. Fined, imprisoned, whipped for disobedience, they see themselves stripped of everything, by people *who made laws to rob under*, and therefore there is no redress. But they writhe under this oppression, and, cowed and miserable though they are, they only submit from the fear that the *missionaries will pray them to death!* They are firmly persuaded that this can be done, and if one is told that he will be "prayed to death," all the terrors of imagination are roused; he retires to his hut chilled with a supernatural fear, lays himself down in resignation to his fate, and in the course of a few weeks, actually sinks into the grave. O, Superstition! Thou friend of missionaries, and terror of barbarians!

There are many, especially in Honolulu, in whom a sense of the monstrous injustice they suffer rankles like a poisonous sting, and the chief sufferer, in pain as in rank, is the royal Kamehameha 3d, who fully feels the mockery of his position. Noble in person, generous to a fault, he has still something of the spirit of his grand old ancestor, Ka-me-ha-me-ha 1st. But he has been from his boyhood so encircled by a complicated web of restrictions and curtailments, which he had not patience to unravel, nor strength to break through, that he has thrown off in disgust all pretensions to royalty, except the name, and has repeatedly declared his intention to abdicate the throne, and live in peaceful retirement. But this would not at all suit the wire-workers; they might not find another king so docile, or so much beloved by his people, and, aware of the general discontent, they dread any change which may serve as an excuse for throwing off their authority. Thus, for a little while they put off the evil day; but the time will soon come when they must yield up their ill-gotten power, and retire into their native insignificance. The farce of royalty acted here reminds me of a play among school-boys, called the "dumb orator," where one boy stands perfectly still and speaks, while another, concealed behind him, makes the motions. Poor Kamehameha makes the motions, but has not a word to say for himself. The real king of the Sandwich Islands is Doctor G. P. Judd, a person of ordinary capacity and attainments, but extraordinary cunning, who came out here from Massachusetts about twenty years ago, attached to some missionary company as physician. Finding the climate so charming, and the opportunities so great, he decided to remain. By degrees he obtained the confidence of the king and principal chiefs, who, looking up to him as a Great Medicine, accepted his advice and assistance in forming a government and making new laws, till at last they found themselves completely in his power. He gave the principal state offices to his fast friends, reserving to himself that of Minister of Finance, which he still holds, and which, for many years, he administered without being responsible to anybody.

At last, so much complaint was made of his expenditure and use of the public monies, that an auditor was appointed, but always a creature of his own, who was very useful, for he did his bidding and formed his shield, at the same time. Meanwhile, his purchases and grants of land were immense, and, it is a matter of record, in the Government House, that he purchased at one time *seventeen thousand acres of land for fifty cents!* But if the king bestows a house and lot upon some faithful old servitor or friend, of whom Mr. Judd does not approve, he is forthwith thrust out of it, and told to go about his business.

The king's allowance is $12,000 per annum. A pitiful sum to keep up his extensive establishment, and gratify his liberality, which is truly royal. But nobody will give him credit, for even his note is not good except it has the signature of the Premier, who of course obeys Mr. Judd. Meanwhile the king is penniless, and must have money; his faithful servant, Mr. Judd, loans it to him at a good rate of interest, and a mortgage on his land; the poor king, never able to pay, sees in despair the heritage of his fathers passing into the hands of his overgrown subject, whose arrogance and possessions hourly increase, until there is nobody in the eyes and mouths of the people, nobody in the estimation of foreigners, nobody, in fact, in all the Sandwich Islands, but Mr. Judd, Minister of Finance. Consuls, Minister of Foreign Relations, Ministers Plenipotentiary, all sink into insignificance, and, if any foreigner, either American or otherwise, hopes to obtain favor, either from government or society, he pays assiduous court, not to the king, nor to the representative of his nation, but to Mr. Judd. The laws and statutes, which were made and compiled under the fostering care of the Minister of Finance, are a complete system of loopholes, through which, if a man chooses, he can slip with a large load upon his back, and even carry off whole plantations, if necessary. What a wonderful adaptation of means to ends.

Freedom of the press is one of the articles guarantied by the Hawaiian constitution. For a long time, the people, especially foreign residents here, have been aware of the pressure of this "Old Man of the Sea" upon their necks, and desirous of unhorsing him. Already their trade was crippled by his exactions, their plantations ruined, and commerce destroyed. They believed their best remedy would be a liberal newspaper, which, by exposing the government, would eventually insure redress. Accordingly, a weekly journal was commenced, which commented pretty freely upon the proceedings of the privy council and king Judd. The latter, wishing to obtain a certain offensive manuscript, invited the compositor to his house, and after plying him freely with wine, offered him three hundred dollars in gold if he would break open a certain trunk, where he knew it was deposited, and obtain it. The compositor, now very tipsy, consented, broke open the trunk, deposited the obnoxious paper in the hands of Mr. Judd, who immediately put him on board a schooner in waiting, and sent him down to Lahaina. The parties robbed, discovering the theft, pursued and brought the culprit back, who, now thoroughly sober, and full of remorse, went with them to Mr. Judd, and exposed the whole plot, which he did not deny, but coolly defied them to lay a finger on the Minister of Finance; and they dared not do it. But these things cannot last. "Curses, not loud, but deep," are showered upon him by the whole business community, and, when they gain a little more strength of numbers, his rule will be abolished, even at the expense of an entire revolution. This, he himself fears and anticipates, and is already bespeaking the forbearance of the planters, by loaning them money to relieve the distress his own measures have brought upon them.

The Kanakas look up to the whites with great reverence and admiration, and they fully believe, that if they had a government like that of the United States, their country would start forward in the race of civilization as rapidly as California has done, of which they have heard so much, and of which they are incessantly talking. There is not a shadow of doubt but, if a few wise and resolute men were found to guide and lead them, that the entire people, with the king at their head, would joyfully aid in the overthrow of the present, and the creation of a new form of government. There is no talk of a discovery of gold mines here, but there are thousands and thousands of acres of rich sugar and coffee lands now lying waste in these islands, in a climate that has not its equal under heaven. All the tropical fruits, and many of the products of the temperate zones, such as corn and all kinds of vegetables, grow here, absolutely without culture or care, except to drop the seed into the earth. The island is covered with cattle, sheep and goats, and horses are so plenty, that almost every native, be he ever so poor, keeps one or two of his own. Millions of fowls are everywhere seen, and thirty hogs can be bought for seventy-five dollars. Nothing ever dies of cold or starvation, and there are no birds or beasts of prey. The scenery of these islands, too, is charming. Lofty hills and lovely dales, towering mountains and smiling valleys, all covered with rich verdure, are delightfully intermingled. Sparkling streams charm eye and ear, while cool breezes wave the most luxuriant foliage. The acacia and rose-geranium grow wild, sweet roses blossom all the year, and immense passion-flowers, indigenous, are the most common of vines. The water is excellent, and the sea is full of fine fish in great variety. What earthly want has man, that cannot here be gratified?

The commercial importance of Honolulu in the future is yet hardly estimated. For many years, it has been the principal and almost the only port for supplying whale ships in this region, and the arrivals are sometimes as many as seven per day. These vessels for three months fitting out for a six, or nine months cruise, necessarily buy largely, and at high prices, because they can buy nowhere else. The merchants also make immense profits by discounting drafts on the United States, the lowest rate being fifteen, and the highest sixty per cent. But when we consider that it lies in the very highway of nations, and of the immense commerce that must necessarily exist between China and the western ports of the United States and Central America, since the wonderful discoveries of gold in California, we can easily foresee a rapid and wonderful increase in the wealth and importance of Honolulu, both from the profitable sale of the island products, and the increase of emigration, attracted by its commercial and agricultural advantages. In a few years it should rival Havana in importance, as it already does in the richness of its dependencies, and become a universal place of resort for all those whose health or leisure induce them to exchange the rainy winters of the Coast for the delicious ones of the Sandwich Islands.

To those accustomed to anything larger than a country village, however, the *society* of Honolulu presents few attractions. Isolated as it is from the rest of the world, with little to excite or interest from without, its members have full leisure to attend to the affairs of their neighbors; and it is irreverently said that a lady long known to the public as Madam Scandal, presides over their tea-tables. She says to the world in general, "If there's a hole in *a'* your coats, I rede ye'll tent it;" and woe to the unlucky wight who has ever so small a rent, for it will be immediately enlarged to admit the seven deadly sins in solid column. It is infinitely amusing to remark in what a different light they look upon strangers, and strangers upon themselves. With them, as in China, all visitors are outside barbarians, while the individual condemned to their society for a few months, bears his penance as patiently as he can, and thanks his stars that it is not forever. "Would that the gods some gift would gie us, to see oursel's as others see us." However, that there are excellent and hospitable people in Honolulu there is no doubt, and perhaps some who go there really *have* ragged coats; besides, they are not so much more severe upon strangers than upon each other; and by visiting the different families in succession, you may obtain the private history of each neighbor, with illustrations and variations; and a very funny melange will be the result.

Mr. Judd's family consider themselves at the head of society, and perhaps their accomplishments would sustain them. Mrs. Judd, I am told, excels in *designing*, the three young ladies play the piano, and, since their father's return from Paris, are scarcely able to speak any English, although they did not accompany him. Their morning toilet has become a *dishabille*, their fancies are *pongchongs*, and instead of wine, they poison people with something they call "Bores (boires) Français." They are all "maids of honor" to her dingy majesty, the queen, who, on reception days, looks like some fat "old Mammy" of the South, displaying "Massa's" children. The children of the present king can never inherit the throne, as the queen is not of noble blood, but by command of the missionaries, was raised from the position of mistress, to that of wife of Kamehameha; thus securing the crown to another branch of the royal family. In fact, all three of the queen's children disappeared immediately after their birth, and have never been heard of since.

Considerable excitement was caused at Honolulu and all the island ports by the arrival of so many Californians as have visited them the present winter, and great military preparations were made to destroy them, if anything like a revolution should be attempted. In the first place, the police was doubled, so as, if possible, to check it in the bud; if that should prove ineffectual, they had at command some eight or ten hundred Kanaka warriors, before whom Bombastes Furioso might have set his boots with impunity. Conceive a mob of natives, of all ages and sizes, ragged and dirty, most of them shoeless, and many without hats, some armed with guns which might go off by chance, more with those which could by no possibility be fired, and you have an idea of the infantry, — cavalry they have none; and their lancers are armed with "sharp sticks," most of them without heads. If this frightful array had failed to lay this phantom rebellion, they would doubtless have resorted to their artillery, only, unfortunately, it was all spiked by the French last year, except that on "Punch Bowl Hill," which commands the town and harbor, and, for that reason, is a greater terror to themselves than anybody else.

Last November, some Kanakas, about thirty in number, who had been confined in the fort for some petty infringement of the laws, made their escape, and, headed by a boy of eighteen, the son of a chief, took the "Hill," turned the guns upon the town, and especially upon Dr. Judd's house, and would have dictated their own terms of surrender, if they could have obtained fire to touch them off. This they were unable to do, and being otherwise unarmed, were forced to yield. The Hawaiian navy is equally formidable with the army; it consists of a vessel of one hundred and fifty tons burden, called the King's Yacht, carrying twelve enormous pop-guns, and manned, besides the commodore, captains, lieutenants, purser, surgeon, midshipmen, &c., by twelve men before the mast! If a revolution should ever be attempted by any parties except the natives, however, they must be prepared to bear nearly the entire brunt of the battle, whatever it may be, for the foreign residents, with few exceptions, will do nothing to commit themselves with the present government, however glad they might be to claim the first advantages of a new one.

The missionaries are very suspicious, and their present policy is to exclude all foreigners from office except themselves, especially if they are popular enough to obtain one. At the election held on the first of January, the "free and independent voters" of Honolulu were forbidden to elect *any white man.* Ministers of the pulpit fulminated their anathemas against those who should dare to vote for one, and a large police force was sent to the polls, who snatched the obnoxious tickets from their hands, and carried those off to the fort who made any resistance; thus illustrating, in a most *forcible* manner, the admirable principles of liberty, so attractively taught by Mr. Judd, *a son of the Pilgrims.* Another point, which at first view would seem a little singular, is the manner of imposing taxes. They have a poll tax, a school tax, horse, mule, donkey, and dog tax, but no tax on *real estate.* The mystery is at once explained, however, by recollecting that the land is nearly all owned by the missionaries, and therefore escapes; while the poor fellow who is so unlucky as to own a donkey to carry his poe to market, must go to the collector's, and pay his tax. Besides those above enumerated, the missionaries oblige all the Kanaka church-members to pay them a weekly tribute. On each Sabbath, they exact a sum in proportion to their means, or to their own power over them; the women always paying the most, and often for themselves and their husbands both, as the men, who never work, have no opportunity of obtaining money, and the women only by the vilest means. This the missionaries are perfectly aware of, and sometimes, in a fit of virtuous indignation, impose an additional fine, on that account. The Rev. T. Coan, at Hilo, Hawaii, said to his congregation a few weeks since, when receiving tribute, "I wish none to pay me the wages of prostitution." "Then, sir," quietly replied one of the women, "you will get nothing, for we have no other money!" To this, of course, there was no reply, *but the tribute was received, as usual.* The same gentleman dismissed a native from the church, for letting a horse to a foreigner on Thursday, to be returned the next Sunday, though the same man had kept a notorious house of ill-fame, for months before, without reproof. It is necessary to "strain at a gnat," occasionally, so as to furnish a high sounding report for the religious community of the United States, and keep up creditably the monstrous humbug which has so long imposed upon them; and I will candidly confess that, in writing these sketches, I feel a hesitancy in exposing its whole length and breadth, lest its enormity should cast a doubt upon the veracity of the whole.

There are in Honolulu about one hundred stores and shops of various kinds, of which probably seventy-five are dry goods and fancy stores. Those foreign merchants who are not missionaries, pay the regular duties imposed on all imports, but the missionary stores receive their goods free from duty, and are in consequence able to undersell all others, and at the same time make a handsome profit. The native women are great and extravagant purchasers; some of them boast of possessing fifty or seventy-five silk and satin dresses; as I have said before, they have only one way of obtaining money, and it is a well known and monstrous fact, that these stores are entirely sustained by the prostitution of the Kanaka women.

We have all heard of the schools established in these islands, and have felt a great interest in their success. These the missionaries have turned to their own account, teaching only the Hawaiian language, which is but a miserable jargon of words, the whole alphabet containing but twelve letters, and susceptible of no improvement. English is only taught in the royal school, where the nobility are educated; if taught to the common people, they would become too intelligent upon the subject of their own position, and the missionaries would lose the influence they possess from speaking the native tongue. The half-castes they do not wish taught at all, and only recently have permitted them to enter their schools. With these people, as with all colored races, an intermixture of blood with the whites improves the intellect, and sharpens the wit;

something by no means desired by their teachers. Within a few years, however, through the efforts of Mr. Reynolds, a benevolent old gentleman from Massachusetts, an excellent charity school has been established, in part supported by the contributions of strangers, and partly by foreign residents, not missionaries. Many attempts have been made to destroy this school, by bribing the teachers, or threatening their expulsion from society, if they persisted in their labors, but all in vain; for, though the position of the female teachers was oftentimes extremely unpleasant, the school has been sustained, and has demonstrated, by the proficiency of its pupils, that they are susceptible of great and rapid improvement. Mr. Reynolds, this venerable philanthropist, has not only succeeded in having the half-castes taught music and other accomplishments, but has himself taught them dancing, though nearly sixty years old, and is regarded by them all as their second and kindest father. Several of his pupils have married wealthy and influential merchants, and are, in fact, almost the only ones recognized in foreign society.

There are but three denominations of Christians now upon the islands, — Presbyterians, Episcopalians, and Catholics; very few indeed of the last, who, by constant annoyance and persecution, have been nearly all driven away. There is no Episcopal clergyman in Honolulu, but the service is read by a gentleman who is soon to take orders. At the "Bethel," or Presbyterian church, the Rev. Mr. Taylor has officiated for some months, in the absence of the Rev. Mr. Damon, the usual occupant of the pulpit. The "Bethel" is always well filled by missionary and foreign residents, well dressed, and very attentive to stereotyped orthodox sermons, untainted by the least suspicion of originality.

The ladies and children come in a kind of wagon to the church, drawn by natives, instead of horses, two of whom (or of *which?*) run before, and one behind. This is the usual way in which they go shopping or to pay visits, and the patient Kanaka throws himself on the ground, quietly waiting till the purchasing or gossipping is finished, and his mistress ready to set out again. At first, this harnessing up of human beings looked a little singular, even after a long residence in a slave state, but, in Honolulu, one soon ceases to be astonished at anything, and rides after a pair of prancing Kanakas with as much composure as if they were ponies. Riding on horseback is the favorite amusement of all colors and classes, and the island roads are admirably suited to its enjoyment. Smooth, hard, and seldom muddy, a canter over them is really delightful, with the fresh sea breeze fanning your cheek, and bearing on its breath the rich perfume of sandal wood and wild flowers.

From Punch Bowl Hill, there is a charming view of the city and bay, which lie in green, and white, and gold, at its foot. At Cocoanut Grove, you may have a gallop on the beach, and see the surf-bathers, who, kneeling on one knee upon a long pointed board, will ride back and forth upon the surf, hours at a time, for your amusement. But the most delightful ride is to the Pa-ra, or precipice, about six miles from Honolulu. The road lies through a lovely valley, filled with charming houses, and gardens embowered in trees, and watered by sparkling rivulets, whose cool murmurs are a continual song of gladness. After a few miles, you

pass into a wilder region; the hills approach each other, the fragrant boughs of the sandal wood almost meet over your head, the rank grass waves undisturbed, and a sudden silence seems to have fallen upon the earth. Deep shadows fill the glen on either side, while now and then a sharp peak shoots up into the sunlight, reflecting back its golden smile. Only the birds have voices, and they call to each other, from their nests among the rich foliage, in happy security. Wilder and narrower, the road gradually ascends, till it is barely wide enough for two horses abreast, when suddenly, without warning, you stand upon the summit of a precipice of fifteen hundred feet sheer descent, and look, after you catch your breath, on to a green and lovely plain below, where the houses look like ant-hills, and men and animals scarcely larger than the industrious insects themselves. A steep and difficult road is cut in the side of the mountain on the right of the Pa-ra, and the view is closed by the sea, which girdles the plain with its blue and restless waters. It was over this frightful precipice that Kamehameha 1st drove his rebellious subjects some forty years ago, and the bones of three thousand men yet lie bleaching at its foot.

The Kanakas are extravagantly fond of riding on horseback, and the women, sitting astride, ride better than the men. There is a fine race-course about two miles from Honolulu, where they try the speed of their horses, almost every evening. On Saturday, their grand gala-day, it is almost dangerous for a lady to attempt to make her way through the streets, and some have been seriously injured by the rash and intemperate riding of the natives against them. Strangers are not allowed the privilege of a hasty gallop, but are forced to take a moderate pace, under the penalty of a visit to the fort, and a fine as large as they dare impose. Strangers, on arriving at the islands, are immediately surrounded by a set of sharpers, who prey upon them while their money lasts, taking every advantage of their inexperience, raising their rents, doubling the price of board, and exacting the highest prices for the smallest service. The servants are a set of organized spies, who report to the government every act and conversation of strangers, so that their thoughts and intentions are as well understood by the privy council as by themselves. Some amusing tricks have been played off upon Mr. Judd, by those who have discovered his system of espionage, which sent him rushing about town on his little poney, in desperate affright.

The usual custom for families and single gentlemen is, to lease a cottage for apartments, and obtain meals at a hotel or boarding-house. There are plenty of natives who ask to be received as servants, and they offer you their wives and female children, *soul and body*, for a few dollars. In fact, most of the men on the island of Oahu support themselves in that way; and as, when they marry *one* of a family of girls, they marry them *all*, their income is often quite handsome. Their half-caste children are nursed with great pride and care by the natives, while those of their own color are often either destroyed, or allowed to perish at their birth, for want of the commonest offices of humanity. Infanticide is not considered wrong among them, and if a child is ill or troublesome, it is put out of the way. For this reason, the proportion of children to the

inhabitants is frightfully small; and I recollect of seeing but two colored infants in Honolulu, where the natives all live out of doors. Even in rainy weather, men, women and children lie around their doors, or by the sides of the streets, stretched on the grass, in every attitude of laziness. Work they will not; they have no trades, no stores, no occupation except to cultivate the Taro, which is merely digging a large, square trench, setting it in rows through it, and letting in the water to cover the roots. If not too lazy, the men can catch plenty of fish just in the harbor; if they are, the women supply the money to buy it, and their larder is furnished.

This excessive indolence is partly the result of climate, partly the simplicity of their wants, which offers no motive for exertion, but more from the debility of disease, which pervades all classes, from the highest to the lowest, the king not excepted, and shows itself in various forms of scrofula and erysipelas, most disgusting to behold. These people are absolutely unable to perform hard labor, if they would; and under no change or form of government, would they become valuable subjects. Whether, eventually, these Islands should be annexed to the United States, or become an independent republic, the introduction of slavery is indispensable to their value The planters have employed natives, who only work when and as much as they choose, and often leave them in the midst of gathering their crops; and they have imported "coolies" from China, who are equally inefficient, and sometimes even more so. If an independent republic should be established, the planters, without slave labor, would be unable to compete either with Manilla, the South American States, or the West Indies, after paying the heavy duties on sugar, their principal product; and most of them now residing in the island have been ruined by the attempt.

Should annexation to the United States ever be contemplated, our government must consider well whether it is worth their while to raise again the vexed question of slavery or anti-slavery on the extreme verge of the western world; and where, too, from the nature of the climate, slavery *will certainly exist*, ere many years be passed. Doubtless, the soil is of great fertility, and no language can describe the beauty of the climate; but have we not millions of acres of uncultivated land, teeming with richness, in various States of the Union, and especially in California? where, at present, quite as much wealth is dug out of its valley farms as out of its gold mines. It is evident to the most casual observer, that the present state of things cannot long continue; the king is greatly diseased, and extremely intemperate, partly from mortification at his own position, and in part because he has been encouraged thus to weaken his own intellect. A few years, and he will pass away, when some great and radical change must take place; as I am persuaded that the native population will unite with the foreign, to prevent the re-establishment of Mr. Judd's authority, if, indeed, they themselves are not extinct ere that time arrives.

The greatest estimate of native population in all the Sandwich Islands at present, is 80,000, while a few years ago, they numbered 150,000 souls. The foreign population is daily increasing; from China and Australia, on the west, while America and the Eastern Continent send large and growing contributions. Few except the missionaries are wealthy, from the restrictions on commerce and agriculture, but all manage to live, from the low price of the absolute necessaries of life, which will sustain them. Many, who afterwards leave, are seduced into remaining until their funds are exhausted, by the promise of profitable employment, and no place is so difficult to escape from in debt. If any person has been in business there, and wishes to leave, he is obliged to advertise his intentions in the government newspaper, for a week before he departs; if he does not, the sheriff is empowered to shut him up in the fort till he pays a fine. If he is in debt, the creditor applies to his consul, who is obliged to refuse him a passport, without which, the creditor forbids the captain of the vessel on which he is going to take him away, under a fine of five hundred dollars. If, in spite of all this, he is detected in the attempt to get away, he is put in the fort, treated as a state prisoner, and put upon the public highway, to work out his debt at *twenty-five cents per day*. The policy of the government evidently is, so to disgust foreigners as to prevent their making the islands their residence.

Mr. Judd, and all connected with it, are rich enough not to risk their present position to increase the commerce or agriculture of the country; and their only safety lies in excluding all foreigners from either office or influence, except creatures of their own. Many a man with too much independence of spirit to suit them, has been crushed out of sight by their persecutions, and forced to leave, or starve. The present state of the Sandwich Islands is that of an un-Christianized despotism, covered by a thick but transparent veil of hypocrisy, which should long ere this have been torn off. That the board of missions is aware of the manner in which its confidence is abused and its aid expended, is not for one moment to be supposed, for the whole missionary community of these islands is interested in keeping it in ignorance; and I am sure the pious and charitable, who have so liberally contributed their substance for what they believed the holiest purposes, would shrink with horror from aiding or abetting such impious hypocrisy; and I trust that all such will read these developments with the same spirit in which they are written, which is that of a love of truth and good faith, superior to all fear of censure.

www.ingramcontent.com/pod-product-compliance
Lightning Source LLC
LaVergne TN
LVHW020638110826
845149LV00004B/1257

9781418190781